This book I respond
being in the church,
dense with atmosphere.
altho I knew the mysterious name and
had seen it on signs for years. Evidently
it was not my time till now, on your
birthday, when I bought it
23 March 2014
love Eugene.

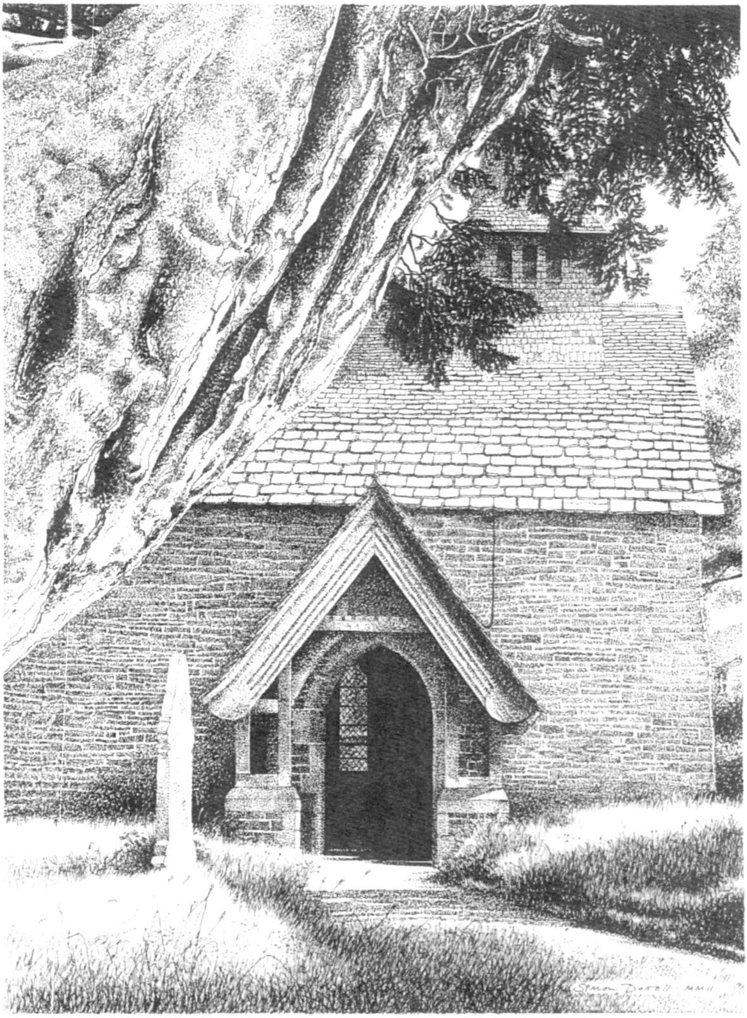

A Discoed Book of Hours

EDWARD STOREY

Foreword by Ronald Blythe

Published on behalf of
The Friends of St Michael's Church, Discoed
by
The Leverett Press
The Leverett
Discoed
Presteigne
LD8 2NW
UK

First published 2013
This collection © Edward Storey, 2013

The author has asserted his rights to be identified as the author of this work in accordance with the Copyright, Designs and Patents Act 1988.

A Discoed Book of Hours
ISBN 978-0-9575375-0-7

Design and layout by Andrew Giles, The Leverett Press
for The Friends of St Michael's Church, Discoed
Set in Arno and Brioso
Printed by Orphans Press, Leominster, UK

Illustrations by Simon Dorrell

Front cover: *St Michael's Church, Discoed – porch from inside*
Frontispiece: *St Michael's Church, Discoed – the Discoed Yew and church porch*
page 45: *St Michael's Church, Discoed*

Also by Edward Storey

Poetry

North Bank Night
A Man in Winter
The Dark Music
A Slant of Light
Last Train to Ely
A Change in the Climate
New and Selected Poems
Lighting a Beacon
Missing the Point
Border Music
Almost a Chime-child

Prose

Portrait of the Fen Country
Four Seasons in Three Countries
The Solitary Landscape
Call it a Summer Country
Spirit of the Fens
Fen, Fire and Flood
The Winter Fens
Fen Country Christmas
In Fen Country Heaven
Letters from the Fens

Autobiography/Biography

Fen Boy First
A Right to Song: A Life of John Clare

Libretti

Katharine of Aragon	(music by Barry Ferguson)
Old Scarlett	(music by Trevor Hold)
No Cross, No Crown	(music by David Twigg)
On a Hill Far Away	(music by David Twigg)

Dedication

*Although several of these poems are dedicated
personally to individuals, I wish the whole collection
to be seen as a tribute to all those who helped to
breathe new life into the church at Discoed.
I specially thank our Rector,
The Reverend Preb. Stephen Hollinghurst,
whose encouragement, support and involvement
opened the door to so many diverse
events and experiences.*

Foreword

by Ronald Blythe

Old friends are not alone in a new place. They bring their company with them. There are fresh prospects for all of us when the change of address card arrives. But Edward Storey is one of those writers who are not supposed to move and *we* were unsettled when *he* settled on the Welsh border, transplanting himself from his native Fens to a foreign land.

His new house abutted onto one of the most ancient addresses imaginable: St Michael's Discoed / Offa's Dyke / Radnorshire / Powys. Take your pick. And then there was this extraordinary border-line of poets: George Herbert, Henry Vaughan, Francis Kilvert, and Thomas Traherne, a company of bards which Edward, for most of his life in Cambridgeshire could never have imagined keeping. And then this old church which was almost in his garden. And an Abrahamic yew tree which made even the church seem new.

Like all of us who love and worship in country churches, I often meet with someone who has especially taken some remote shrine in hand and brightened it. This is what the poet Edward Storey has done here, and

A DISCOED BOOK OF HOURS celebrates what
he and his neighbours have accomplished. It is
a volume that is both elegiac and full of the future,
a guide-book to Time in a small Welsh village.
A meditation on what is long-lived.

I cannot think of a better way for a simple country
church to speak to those who push open its ancient
doors than through these poems.

Introduction

In 1999 I knew the time had come for me to leave my native lowlands of East Anglia and try a different part of the country for a few years. I never imagined it would mean crossing the border into Wales. But that is what happened and, on the hottest July day of that summer, my wife and I found ourselves in the small hamlet of Discoed hidden in a quiet corner of Radnorshire (now Powys). It was here I re-discovered the true value of time and peace, helped largely by living next door to the church and churchyard, in which stood a 5000-year-old yew tree.

As a writer, I wondered how easily I would adapt, not only to the spacious and beautiful landscape of hills, valleys and sheep, but also to a community that was still unknown to me. I need not have worried. The few houses scattered about the narrow lanes gave us neighbours as friendly as the scenery.

When we joined the small devoted congregation of St Michael's Church we soon learned that the old building was in need of urgent restoration if it was to continue as a place of worship, so we became part of a committee determined to raise the money needed for repairs. Perhaps we could help.

This collection is, therefore, a personal celebration of the days, seasons and festivities that became part of our new life. Some of the earliest poems refer to pews no longer in the nave and a roof that is now leak-proof. Later poems speak of what was found under the floor when the pews were removed – the remains of villagers who were here three hundred years ago. Towards the end of the restoration work these bones were re-interred in the chancel and the Discoed bell rang for them as it still rings for us. Above all, these poems commemorate the life of a shepherd's church on the border of Wales which has been a witness for our belief for centuries. I am grateful to the Friends of St Michael's for so much.

Apart from twelve previously unpublished poems, the others have been selected from earlier collections written mainly for the church: *Lighting a Beacon* (2003); *Missing the Point* (2004), and *Border Music* (2006). Five poems from *Almost a Chime-child* (2010) have also been included because they are part of the story.

The proceeds from this publication will go towards the replacement of a small stained-glass roundel window in the west-end wall of the church.

E.S. 2013.

Contents

9	The Invitation
10	Petition from the Parish
11	Here, Moonlight Too
12	A Place Like This
13	The Visitors' Book
14	From a Vestry Book
15	I'd Come Back Tomorrow if I Could
16	Neighbourhood Watch
17	Waiting
18	The Window
19	Evening Service
20	Communion
21	Afterwards
22	Faith
23	A Yew Tree's Testament
24	A Friend's Goodnight to the Yew Tree

25	The Formula
26	An Unexpected Visitor
27	From Over the Wall
29	A Skeleton in the Nave
31	Mourning the Neighbours We Did Not Know
32	The Rehearsal
33	Christmas Eve
34	The Discoed Bell
35	A Shepherd Contemplates
36	A Last Supper at Discoed
37	A Good-Friday Incident
39	When Shadows Are Too Deep
40	Pause
41	The Return
43	St Michael's Guests
44	A Valediction

The Invitation

A man was strimming the churchyard grass –
Hay-smell, apple-and-nut smell
On the hottest day of the year.

We had just moved into the house next door
Where only a low stone wall
Divided the living from the dead.

Beyond the valley, hills were as pale as sand-dunes.
They could have been anywhere
Other than this land fashioned by soft rain.

Then evening came and, in that calm hour
Between day ending and darkness claiming
Its share of the earth, it felt like home.

How easily we forget the past.
The country I had known was now so far away
I was convinced I had been born again.

Crossing the border into Wales
Was more than defining a boundary,
More than dividing the living and dead.

Between the potent smell of drying grass
And stars opening their petals in night's meadows,
Were older voices saying: *Now sit with us.*

Petition from the Parish

Much has been expected of you, Michael,
protecting more churches in Wales
than any saint, except the Virgin Mary.
But of all your tasks, there is one place
for which we ask more than an angel's eye –
our own St Michael's, dwarfed by a tree
That was full-grown three thousand years
Before a Christian stone was laid upon this hill.

It is a simple place if one sees only walls
And adds a stained-glass window at a later date.
Here are no fancy decorations or vain monuments;
even the altar would not have looked conspicuous
in the Upper Room. Our focus is on faith.
A doll's-house porch gathers the evening light
stooping beneath an aching roof
as pagan jackdaws vandalise the spire.

Stepping inside you'd meet the grateful ghosts
who worshipped here when church was more
than ritual or a landlord's threat.
Those families farmed and paid their tithes,
preserving somewhere for their dead to rest.
If Jacob had woken here and not in Luz,
his cry would still have been: *This is none other
than God's house, and this the gate of heaven.*

Here, Moonlight Too

But for a few, the moon would have no walls
to lean on, no latticed glass through which
on autumn nights to pry when hills
are lunar silent. One day there might be stones
too overgrown with grass to show
whose names were left here as a testament
to other times, yet they could not begin
to prove what power once dwelt within
this gentle place. These walls are more
than weight or measurement, the roof
more than a barrier to wind or rain. So far
those questions have not been asked
so this is still God's house. Here there is peace
as sacred as the privilege which allows
all who will enter without pride or wealth.
Here moonlight too must kneel, creep in
through open doors or windows to partake
of love's communion in the radiant dark.

A Place Like This

Inside, we are a breath between centuries,
an uneasy shuffle in the creaking pews,
the conscience pricked as always by a thorn.

Of all who once knelt here, only a few
are now remembered. The walls
are mostly bare of their memorials.

Strangers *en route* to somewhere else
pause to absorb the silences of prayer
then sign the visitors' book and go.

A place like this is refuge to all ghosts
and holds their secrets in its hands
as wine held briefly in a cup.

Outside, twelve jackdaws argue with a crow
and sunlight helps regenerate a yew
familiar with each quest and ritual.

One day it could unite some distant creed
with what now stumbles blindly in the dark,
hoping the answers do not come too late.

The Visitors' Book

Not for autographs or a hotel register
but a book of moments, where the names
of those who briefly came to share
the meaning of this place, are left
for all to read who follow after –
pilgrims, walkers from Offa's Dyke,
and some who, out of curiosity,
paused to hear what empty pews
and bare walls had to say, not even sure
of what they might themselves believe.

Others stayed longer to feel the ages
now absorbed by stones –
the lingering past that will not go away,
the hidden truths that still survive
though darkness threatens to destroy.
Here also are the signatures of those
who sought us out, from Norway,
Canada, New Zealand and the USA,
travellers from around the world
who came to know us for a day.

So history is made. Before we go
Perhaps there is a page we too should sign.
How else will those who follow know we came?

From a Vestry Book

It may not have crossed your mind, Ann Rogers,
That you would be remembered, but here you are,
Two centuries on as part of our memory.
We do not know how plain or beautiful you were.
How shy or bold, only that you were once
A servant-girl with a wage of a guinea a year.

There is a curiosity to know much more,
Not out of pity or to make you blush –
Though one fact leaves you modestly exposed
When we are told that annually you received
A pair of stays, three shifts, one pettycote
and three handkerchiefs.   Who paid for those?

And what will be said of this year's labourers?
We go about our tasks in different ways
Filling our days with deeds we trust will last
For there is little that a vestry book can say
That is more accurate or eloquent
Than what we leave behind us when we go.

I'd Come Back Tomorrow if I Could

Nearly ninety-years old
And her memory fresher
Than yesterday's newspapers.

Not only its headlines
But the small paragraphs
That no one younger would remember.

Having left when she was ten
She still knew who her neighbours were
And how she came to Sunday-school.

The church was getting colder
Yet she had more to tell
Of life here eighty years ago.

She then asked if she could see
The house where she was born and was surprised
To find not much had changed –

Except the room itself:
The bed's not where it was! For which
The owners felt they should apologise.

*But I'd come back tomorrow if I could
And die in that same bed. When you have lived
Somewhere like this, it's in your blood.*

Neighbourhood Watch

She arrives three times a week
To take afternoon tea with her husband,
Sitting close to his grave on the stone seat
Placed there for that reason.

She brings his dog – now her dog –
Who settles near his master's feet.
The grass around the rim is cut to look
As cosy as their favourite fireside rug.

She stays almost an hour,
Breathing her thoughts, a silent tete-a-tete.
Convinced he's listening, she says again
How much she misses him at nights.

Then, when it's time to go,
She packs away the unseen cups and plates
Which they once shared when love for them
Was always so complete.

She does not know or care
If she is watched. This hour is intimate
For she is in that private world
Where hearts still quicken when hands touch.

It is not her devotion that is strange
But the cold stare of those who wait
To see, if one day, she might cry
And leave a crushed, wet Kleenex on the seat.

Waiting

(for James Roose-Evans)

. . . prayer is more
Than an order of words . . .
Or the sound of the voice praying.   T.S. Eliot

Only one person present,
And a bee quietly beating
Against latticed glass,
Preferring the light outside
To an empty church.

But, for one kneeling alone,
There is the same expectancy
As for a formal liturgy,
The same demands being made
In an inadequate language.

Why is prayer so obstinate,
Or the mind a closed door?
It is the bee's fault, droning
Like a persistent doubt
Trapped in the heart.

Then silence, as if all the wings
Of the universe have been stilled,
Or the bee has found a way out.
Without asking, peace comes,
Like light at the touch of a switch.

The Window

Light hath no tongue, but is all eye.   John Donne.

The answer is there – peace
Transcending the sorrow of the cross,
Radiance making his suffering bearable.

Only the mother gives cause for grief,
Her face now aged beyond her years;
His death more painful than his birth.

Those who still comfort her
Have gained a look of wonder in their eyes,
As if they've seen beyond stained-glass.

Their robes show colours so intense
Each segment of the window is a flame
Blazing through winter's dark.

When language fails
And our hearts' voices break,
The word will still be heard through light.

Evening Service

(for Stephen)

As always, an air of expectancy
As we approach the door –
The usual few, perhaps, and someone else
We take for granted will be there.

If graves had windows, we are sure
Curtains would twitch from those
Who will be absent (not from choice)
To see who's late, or what we wear.

The bell's dry throat again invites
The neighbourhood to evening prayer.
Mostly we gather two by two
As if we're counted in by Noah.

The ark is quiet. Within an hour
We shall become one body through one bread.
And from the spire a blackbird sings
For all the living and all the dead.

Communion

(for David and Judy)

The chalice makes the same journey
From hand to lip that it has made
Through four hundred years of neighbours –

Shepherds, weavers, millers and ploughmen
Whose hopes met at this table.
Few went away empty.

We too must kneel, knowing this act
Is more than ceremony
As hands reach out to take the cup.

We do so in remembrance,
Rising only to make room
For others who will come

With their own hunger,
Leaving their shadows on grey stones
As forgiving as His cross.

Afterwards

(for Dorothy and Dilwyn)

We leave in twos and threes,
Restored and talking more at ease;
Even our laughter is appropriate.

The porch is now our exit,
The hills an altar for the sun's last light.
Worship is not over yet.

We are reminded that our years
Are only seconds in God's eyes,
A holy blink between earth's day and night.

Passing the yew tree (and those
Already at their rest), we learn
Leaving is only arriving somewhere else.

Faith

(for Beth)

A man is cutting the churchyard grass
Which is headstone high.
He has waited until the daffodils
Reached their season to die.

Underneath are those neighbours who mowed
In summers long past.
Most of their unsung labours now
Are forgotten or lost.

Older by far are the Radnorshire hills
Where low shadows strim
Each meadow and stone, as they will
For another millennium .

Nothing can change the pattern of death
Or wonder of birth
As Easter sheds from a flowering bough
Its pollen of faith.

A Yew Tree's Testament

(for John and Annie)

How could this tree's biography ever be written?
Had sight reached beyond boundaries it might
Have watched the Hebrew's flight from slavery
Long before David's psalms were sung.
Closer to where its roots were struck in Wales,
It saw the earliest shepherds come
With weavers and harpists, their eyes bewildered by
The first conjuring tricks of Spring.

Now it looks on another world of slaves
Which may have measured space
But failed to lengthen hours by an inch.
This tree has written its own testament,
And neither it nor any dying star can say
Where the next birth-seed will be sown.

Yet why should we stop singing?
We too are freed by music that breaks chains
And, for the split second of a millennium,
Join in the dance to blossom, root, and stone.
The footprint we have left upon the moon
Is only one more note in Time's own song.

A Friend's Goodnight to the Yew Tree

(for Kirsty Williams)

Did the tree blush when you touched it that night?
I'm sure its trunk took on a redder glow
Than when the sun's last rays coloured its bark.
Who else could have made its cheeks so bright?
Not Nefertiti, whose imperious lips
Might not have smiled at your impulsive kiss.

While Time is still earth's pendulum
Five thousand years are nothing in its eyes,
And she, who once was beautiful must now
Adopt your gentler countenance to gaze
Upon a tree so old it can recall
All lovers who were young and Eden-wise.

Some distant age may wonder why this bough
Blushed so. Maybe (like any flattered man)
It half-believed the touch was deftly meant.
The truth's a secret we shall never know,
But what was done between the light and dark
No sun or moon can ever take away.

The Formula

There is in God (some say)
A deep but dazzling darkness.   Henry Vaughan

There was no rain to prove
The chemistry of a rainbow
But it was there, arched
Against a blue glass sky,
Defying earth's natural laws
Or the wind's wish to blow it away.

It appeared, I thought,
As a forgotten face at the window
Or as a voice on the telephone
Dead from a line brought down,
Unlikely if not impossible.
Some would call this a miracle.

It is the same with prayer,
If mystery is denied us
How can we outreach the stars
To touch the hem of space?
There is no other formula
To feel the voltage of His fire.

An Unexpected Visitor

(for Sally Evans)

Nothing unusual in our ritual –
A hymn, the gospel, and the priest
Testing our consciences again,
Followed by intercessions and the Peace
Before sharing Communion;
Low sunlight peering in from evening's hill.

But our devotions were distracted by
A swallow weaving anthems overhead –
A thread of incense for the inner eye
Reminding us of what Bede said:
We too are birds just passing through
A place the heart persuaded us to try.

We enter and we leave, but cannot say
Why our own wing-beats still give hope
Even when words are struggling to pray.
Yet these are moments we shall keep
Long after migrant birds have gone,
Long after the singing has died away.

From Over the Wall

(for Dilwyn and Mike)

Between the spire and the yew
Time moves and yet is strangely still,
As if somewhere the seconds hold
The power to stop a spinning world.

We see a neighbour come each day
To check the unlocked church is well.
He takes his cap off in the porch
Then quietly lifts the ancient latch.

For him the duty is a joy,
Part of his yearly chronicle.
Seasons will never change his mind
Or slow the labours of his hand.

Another neighbour cuts the grass
When his own daily tasks are done,
Content that in the evening light
The churchyard looks immaculate.

And there are those who come to pray
When no one else is there to see,
And those who cannot understand
The purpose of this hallowed ground.

Some come to hear musicians play
And love to think the walls might save
Sweet echoes for the pilgrims who
Will tread this path in years from now.

For them, and all who cross the space
Between the spire and the yew,
Something will make them pause and be
Wiser because of church and tree.

A Skeleton in the Nave

(for an unknown villager)

Exposed to summer in your shallow grave,
Your skull cocked to one side as though
Listening through a keyhole for news
Of Judgement Day, you must have heard
A thousand dry-bone sermons in this nave
Where later worshippers staked out their pews,
Oblivious of your sleeping underneath.

Alone in those long silences between
Each Sunday's condemnation could you feel
Roots fidgeting around old broken stones
When earlier neighbours gathered on this brow?
Do ghosts have shadows, or bones explain
Why skies are always dark, and the moon's
Forever in eclipse above the yew?

Would your eyes blink at sunlight now
Or nostrils twitch to smell the incense
After rain when grass has just been cut?
Would ears still heed the bell-tongue's begging prayer –
Or not? With you there's nothing left to show
Your name or rank, no title, gender, date
To say if you were shepherd, wife, or squire.

Tomorrow we shall bury you again, your day
Of freedom from eternity well-spent, your bones
Re-settled in a place new tributes will enhance.
And, just a few tomorrows after that,
We too will learn what you already know –
But, unlike you, we may not get the chance
Of one more sigh before the last goodnight.

Mourning the Neighbours We Did Not Know

(for David Hiam, who tolled the bell.)

Now, after three hundred years, we come
To toll a funeral-bell and re-inter
The bones a different generation saw
Buried beneath the cold floor of the nave.

Maybe there was no bell that long ago
To tell why they had gathered there;
It was our task to solemnize their grave
And mourn the neighbours we would never know.

Was it by chance they had to wait
Until the restoration of a church
Proved that centuries do not separate
Communities? Most of what's lost
Is only something death puts out of reach.

All future is soon buried with the past
And in another age this bell will toll
For those who'll have a longer tale to tell.

The Rehearsal

(for Carole, Sharon and Eleanor)

So fair a fancy few would weave
In these years! Yet, I feel,
If someone said ...   Thomas Hardy

Late afternoon and the church empty
But for a group of neighbours
Rehearsing their Christmas play;
Not yet word-perfect but convinced
Their words are making history.

So far no props or costumes
Help them to portray
The characters they must become,
But soon the chancel is a barn,
The crib and cattle real for them.

Next week when Mary's child
Sleeps in the stable-lantern's glow,
The villagers will gather round
To wait in their own candlelight,
Hoping it might be so.

Christmas Eve

(for Angela)

We went alone in the dark
To the cold church, knelt
On the bare stones – for what?

There were no angels, no
Shepherds or wise-men arriving,
No sign of the animals.

There was no manger either,
Mary wept by a cross
In a stained-glass window.

But we spoke our words
And let the silence follow,
Two minds as one, knowing

The moment for which we'd gone
Was already there.   It was the child
Who was waiting.

We presented our gifts –
Love, gratitude, prayer,
Then walked into the night

Led by a star.

The Discoed Bell

(for Sue)

This ancient bell of Discoed rings
With all the bells of Christendom,
Not for one year but all the years
Since Christ was born in Bethlehem.

Second by second, note by note,
It still proclaims the faith of those
For whom that star will never set,
The door of loving never close.

Across the fields and silent hills
It is the constant voice of prayer,
The heart-beat of a holy place,
A witness in the winter air.

It echoes now for all that's passed,
It welcomes all that is to be;
A promise in a tower of stone,
The singing fruit of God's own tree.

Ring out, old bell, remind the world
That we still celebrate the birth
Of One who, in a single night,
Changed the history of the earth.

(this poem has also been set as a hymn by the composer Trevor Hold.)

A Shepherd Contemplates

It was not the first time he had seen
The long-backed hill heavy with snow
But this year was different.

He saw it now as the last polar bear
Stranded alone on the earth
Dying under the pelt of winter.

Whatever tomorrow might bring
He felt that morning would never again
Be part of his yearly routine.

The threat to his own survival
Made him as vulnerable
As anything under the sun.

All planets die. But on days like this
He longed for his to stand still,
To avoid what was waiting to come.

 Feeling the cold in his hands
Ache more in his heart, he saw
Earth was as fragile as man.

Yet, when you cannot turn back the clock,
What can anyone do but hope
And hold on!

A Last Supper at Discoed

(for Debbie)

Was it no more than chance
That thirteen of us sat that night
Around a table in the church
Low-lit by candlelight?

Did we imagine then
We had gone to the Upper Room
As a few invited friends
To share a meal with them?

Yet each of us broke bread
Which we passed to our next-door guest,
Followed by wine blessed to become
Part of the solemn feast.

Each word, each glance, each touch
So quietly personal, we all
Became one body in the gift
Love made acceptable.

Walking back home we were
Amazed to think how close
We'd come to that first sacrament,
The sacrifice, the cross.

A Good-Friday Incident

(for Ronald Blythe)

At first I did not see him on the hill
Or would have turned and gone another way,
But when he asked if he could keep me company
I could not find it in me to say no.

His eyes had similarities with ones
I'd seen before (though we had never met).
His voice, too, was familiar, more
Like a friend's or brother's.

He said: *This hill reminds me of a place*
Where, many years ago, a young man died.
His life too short, some followers thought,
To prove that love can cure overnight;

Three years will never be enough for those
Whose faith relies on miracles.   Could not
One person in his time achieve
More than a longer life-span might?

We should be asking not how short our stay
But what a life is worth before it dies,
Consider what I said about the fields' wildflowers . . .

He smiled to see my look of disbelief
Then touched my arm and slowly walked away,
While all around stones blossomed into lilies,

White as snow.

When Shadows Are Too Deep

(for Anna)

It is from what we do not see
We learn to see; the face
Hidden by cloth gradually revealed
When the reflection of light
   Appears in darkness.

In that surprised dimension
We comprehend what's almost there –
Features half-recognised, eyes
Full of compassion, a brow
   Heavy with sorrow.

Sometimes we stand too close
To accept the obvious,
The white on shadows far too deep
To let the subtleties of night
   Explain such mysteries.

But peel back the borrowed shroud
And we shall find the end
Is the beginning, and the flame
Alive in the dark is love –
   As it always was.

(on the painting 'Jesus is Placed in the Tomb' by Lois Hopwood)

Pause

(for Charles MacCarthy)

Hold it!   Now look again.
That is the moment when it all went wrong,
There in the dark, where only eyes communicate
And a finger, like a sign-post, points
Towards a man trading a traitor's kiss.

Even a whisper can give the game away,
One syllable make a scene catch fire
Or halve the midnight price of silver.
Conspirators are trained to hold their tongues.

So freeze that frame where
Treachery changed everything.
We cannot let the film rush on until we know
Tomorrow will expose their shame
And weeping Judas hangs from his own tree.

(based on Charles's painting 'The Betrayal of Jesus')

The Return

    We are home!
After a year's journey into the unknown
    We are back where we belong –
Under the safe rafters, in a harbour of stone;
Not as exiles or a prodigal son
But as travellers home from abroad
Having lodged at a wayside inn
    Called 'The Upper Room'.

    There were days
When we feared we might never live to see
    Our glistening spire or roof
Freed from captivity. We, too, had to learn
How hard it is to forfeit a place
And ease the human need to yearn
    For lost paradise.

    Yet Time passed.
The daily tapping of the tilers ceased
    And, one by one, the craftsmen's
Tasks came to an end. St Michael's was released
From its scaffolding. Rejoicing would come
When we heard again the Discoed Bell
Calling, calling, calling us home
    To a house thrice-blessed.

    Love-given,
We gratefully receive and then bequeath
    Our faith to others, for we
Are but mortal moments of immortal breath,
The link between what was and is to be -
A church restored, made whole, made one,
Where all may share our sanctuary,
    This Gate of Heaven.

(this poem was written specially for the Service of Re-dedication held on Sunday, 26th October, 2008, conducted by the Revd. Stephen Hollinghurst. The Address was given by Dr Ronald Blythe.)

St Michael's Guests

(for David Ponsford)

Beyond each spoken word and silent prayer
These walls make room for music and the sound
Of harmony accompanying an air
Born of soul-longing, sadness, or desire
To praise. Who has not felt their deepest wound
Healed by a melody, their heart catch fire
Because a song re-kindled thoughts of one
Who shared the purpose of each shining note?
When love is all, no one need feel alone
Where window-sills are lit by candlelight.
St Michael's welcomes to this sacred place
Art, music, poetry and the skills of those
Who, through their craft, bring glory to a house
Already blessed with earthly paradise.

(with the restoration of the church and the removal of the pews, we were able to extend our fund-raising activities to include exhibitions and more ambitious concerts.

We are grateful to the many professional musicians and artists who have generously brought their talents to St Michael's.)

A Valediction

For all who lay under the stars.   Edward Thomas

The churchyard is full of daffodils again
Where several of the headstones lean
To eavesdrop on the words
Which never can be shared
Beyond the secret of our memories.
Others have not worn time so easily,
The lettering more difficult to read.

The one for whom I first gave thought
When I arrived to be her neighbour
Was Catherine Edwards, who died
Two centuries ago.   And yet,
Because I liked her name,
I felt I must have known her once
And owed her my remembrance.

Others I came to know, sharing their laughter
In early days when I desired to be
Part of their company.   They too
Belong to memory, yet still for me
Are never far away.   Their stones
Stand upright in the sun, their names
Alive again with these bright daffodils –

Alan, Mary, Judy, Brian and *John*
Who blessed this gentle hillside
With a presence that will never be
Forgotten.   We live for them
Hoping that in years to come
Our modest book of hours
Will honour their requiem.

(this poem was written before our neighbour Sadie Cole was buried in the churchyard on 12th December 2012.)